# SACREDSPACE

## for Lent 2013

# SACREDSPACE

## for Lent 2013

from the website www.sacredspace.ie

The Irish Jesuits

ave maria press AmP notre dame, indiana

# acknowledgment

The publisher would like to thank Brian Grogan, S.J., for his kind assistance in making this book possible. Correspondence with the Sacred Space team can be directed to feedback@sacredspace.ie where comments or suggestions related to the book or to www.sacredspace.ie, will always be welcome.



Published under license from Michelle Anderson Publishing Pty Ltd., in Australia.

---



Founded in 1865, Ave Maria Press is a ministry of the United States Province of Holy Cross.

www.avemariapress.com

ISBN-10: 1-59471-339-1 ISBN-13: 978-1-59471-339-2

Cover design by Andy Wagoner.

Text design by Kristen Hornyak Bonelli.

Printed and bound in the United States of America.

# how to use this book

During this Lenten season, we invite you to make a sacred space in your day. Spend ten minutes praying here and now, wherever you are, with the help of a prayer guide and scripture chosen specially for each day. Every place is a sacred space, so you may wish to have this little book available at any time or place during the course of the day: in your desk at work, while traveling, on your bedside table, in your purse or jacket pocket. . . . Remember that God is everywhere, all around us, constantly reaching out to us, even in the most unlikely situations. When we know this, and with a bit of practice, we can pray anywhere.

The following pages will guide you through a session of prayer stages:

Something to think and pray about each day this week

The Presence of God

Freedom

Consciousness

The Word (leads you to the daily Lenten scripture and provides help with the text)

Conversation

Conclusion

It is most important to come back to these pages each day of the week as they are an integral part of each day's prayer and lead to the scripture and inspiration points.

Although written in the first person, the prayers are for "doing" rather than for reading out. Each stage is a kind of exercise or meditation aimed at helping you to get in touch with God and God's presence in your life.

We hope that you will join the many people around the world praying with us in our sacred space.

# The Presence of God

Bless all who worship you, almighty God,
from the rising of the sun to its setting:
from your goodness enrich us,
by your love inspire us,
by your Spirit guide us,
by your power protect us,
in your mercy receive us,
now and always.

# february 13–16

Something to think and pray about each day this week:

**Taking the Cross**

It is the start of Lent, the season that leads to our commemoration of the passion and resurrection of Jesus. Jesus said, "Take up your cross" (Mark 8:34, Luke 9:23). It is not something you go looking for in faraway places. Sooner or later the Lord hands us a cross, and our job is to recognize it. For each of us, there are events that make a difference. The sorrowful mysteries are different for each of us. Maybe it is a meeting with a friend, a lover, or an enemy. Maybe it is a sickness or a triumph. We try to see our lives through the eyes of faith, with a confidence that God in his Providence can draw good out of the most awful and unwelcome happenings.

**The Presence of God**

'I stand at the door and knock,' says the Lord.
What a wonderful privilege
that the Lord of all creation desires to come to me.
I welcome His presence.

**Freedom**

Lord, grant me the grace to be free from the excesses of this life.
Let me not get caught up with the desire for wealth.
Keep my heart and mind free to love and serve you.

**Consciousness**

'There is a time and place for everything,' as the saying goes.
Lord, grant that I may always desire to spend time in your presence. To hear your call.

**The Word**

God speaks to each one of us individually. I need to listen to what he is saying to me. (Please turn to your scripture on the following pages. Inspiration points are there should you need them. When you are ready, return here to continue.)

**Conversation**

The gift of speech is a wonderful gift.
May I use this gift with kindness.
May I be slow to utter harsh words, hurtful words, and words spoken in anger.

4

**Conclusion**

Glory be to the Father, and to the Son,
and to the Holy Spirit,
As it was in the beginning, is now and ever shall be,
World without end. Amen.

**Wednesday 13th February,**
**Ash Wednesday** **Matthew 6:1–6**

Jesus said to his disciples, "Beware of practicing your piety before others in order to be seen by them; for then you have no reward from your Father in heaven. So whenever you give alms, do not sound a trumpet before you, as the hypocrites do in the synagogues and in the streets, so that they may be praised by others. Truly I tell you, they have received their reward. But when you give alms, do not let your left hand know what your right hand is doing, so that your alms may be done in secret; and your Father who sees in secret will reward you. And whenever you pray, do not be like the hypocrites; for they love to stand and pray in the synagogues and at the street corners, so that they may be seen by others. Truly I tell you, they have received their reward. But whenever you pray, go into your room and shut the door and pray to your Father who is in secret; and your Father who sees in secret will reward you."

- Given the very different climate that exists in today's world, Jesus might well say the opposite, "Pray in public. Let your light shine before others so that, seeing you pray, they might be drawn to God!"

**Thursday 14th February** **Luke 9:22–25**

Jesus said to his disciples: "The Son of Man must undergo great suffering, and be rejected by the elders, chief priests, and scribes, and be killed, and on the third day be raised." Then he said to them all, "If any want to become my followers, let them deny themselves and take up their cross daily and follow me. For those who want to save their life will lose it, and those who lose their life for my sake will save it. What does it profit them if they gain the whole world, but lose or forfeit themselves?"

- Taking up one's cross is not a matter of simply putting up with the headaches and ordinary troubles of life, but of not being ashamed of Jesus, and being prepared to be true followers with all the dangers, even possible martyrdom, that it implies.
- Trying to save one's own skin by denying Jesus will only result in the loss of eternal life, intimate union with God.

**Friday 15th February** **Matthew 9:14–15**

Then the disciples of John came to him, saying, "Why do we and the Pharisees fast often, but your disciples do not fast?" And Jesus said to them, "The wedding guests cannot mourn as long as the bridegroom is with them, can they? The days will come when the bridegroom is taken away from them, and then they will fast."

- Matthew understands fasting to be a sign of mourning. Jesus compares his disciples to wedding guests who rejoice while he, the bridegroom, is still with them.
- But after he leaves them, they will experience many tribulations; and therefore, they will have good reasons for fasting.

**Saturday 16th February** **Luke 5:27–32**

After this he went out and saw a tax collector named Levi, sitting at the tax booth; and he said to him, "Follow me." And he got up, left everything, and followed him. Then Levi gave a great banquet for him in his house; and there was a large crowd of tax collectors and others sitting at the table with them. The Pharisees and their scribes were complaining to his disciples, saying,

"Why do you eat and drink with tax collectors and sinners?" Jesus answered, "Those who are well have no need of a physician, but those who are sick; I have come to call not the righteous but sinners to repentance."

- Jesus refers in an ironic tone to the scribes and Pharisees as "righteous"; by contrast, Jesus is the "doctor" who brings true righteousness (union with God) through his teaching and healings.
- Self-righteousness is not confined to people who lived at the time of Christ!

# february 17–23

Something to think and pray about each day this week:

**Strength of the Desert**

Jesus went into the desert as an unknown young carpenter from Nazareth, with thirty years of hidden life behind him. After the desert, he returned to Galilee "with power of the Spirit in him," and started to preach. Quickly he became a public figure, but he loved to withdraw to desert or mountain to recharge his energies by prayer. He moved forward like any of us, with no sure knowledge of what was to happen him. His life was shaped by the Spirit driving him forward, but molded also by the accidents of his life, the enthusiasm of some of his listeners, and the resistance of others. He had a sense of where God was calling him—"I am sent to cast fire on the earth"—and of the joy he felt in this vocation—"My meat is to do the will of him who sent me." After the quiet life of Nazareth, Jesus's public life was tumultuous. If we are to do justice to his humanity, we must accept that he did not know what would happen next, only that this was where God wanted him to be.

**The Presence of God**

Jesus waits silent and unseen to come into my heart.
I will respond to His call.
He comes with His infinite power and love.
May I be filled with joy in His presence.

**Freedom**

I ask for the grace
to let go of my own concerns

and be open to what God is asking of me, to let myself be guided and formed by my loving Creator.

**Consciousness**

Knowing that God loves me unconditionally,
I can afford to be honest about how I am.
How has the last day been, and how do I feel now?
I share my feelings openly with the Lord.

**The Word**

I read the Word of God slowly, a few times over, and I listen to what God is saying to me. (Please turn to your scripture on the following pages. Inspiration points are there should you need them. When you are ready, return here to continue.)

**Conversation**

Remembering that I am still in God's presence,
I imagine Jesus himself standing or sitting beside me,
and say whatever is on my mind, whatever is in my heart,
speaking as one friend to another.

**Conclusion**

Glory be to the Father, and to the Son,
and to the Holy Spirit,
As it was in the beginning, is now and ever shall be,
World without end. Amen.

**Sunday 17th February,**
**First Sunday of Lent** **Luke 4:1–8, 13**

Jesus, full of the Holy Spirit, returned from the Jordan and was led by the Spirit in the wilderness, where for forty days he was tempted by the devil. He ate nothing at all during those days, and when they were over, he was famished. The devil said to him, "If you are the Son of God, command this stone to become a loaf of bread." Jesus answered him, "It is written, 'One does not live by bread alone.'" Then the devil led him up and showed him in an instant all the kingdoms of the world. And the devil said to him, "To you I will give their glory and all this authority; for it has been given over to me, and I give it to anyone I please. If you, then, will worship me, it will all be yours." Jesus answered him, "It is written, 'Worship the Lord your God, and serve only him.'"

When the devil had finished every test, he departed from him until an opportune time.

- Lord, you deliberately told your disciples of these temptations—how else would they have known?
- Can I put words to my own temptations, the weaknesses or wickedness that I'm most attracted to?
- Can I see my temptations as you did, against the backdrop of the vocation to which you call me?

**Monday 18th February  Matthew 25:31–40**

Jesus said to his disciples, "When the Son of Man comes in his glory, and all the angels with him, then he will sit on the throne of his glory. All the nations will be gathered before him, and he will separate people one from another as a shepherd separates the sheep from the goats, and he will put the sheep at his right hand and the goats at the left. Then the king will say to those at his right hand, 'Come, you that are blessed by my Father, inherit the kingdom prepared for you from the foundation of the world; for I was hungry and you gave me food, I was thirsty and you gave me something to drink, I was a stranger and you welcomed me, I was naked and you gave me clothing, I was sick and you took care of me, I was in prison and you visited me.' Then the righteous will answer him, 'Lord, when was it that we saw you hungry and gave you food, or thirsty and gave you something to drink? And when was it that we saw you a stranger and welcomed you, or naked and gave you clothing? And when was it that we saw you sick or in prison and visited you?' And the king will answer them, 'Truly I tell you, just as you did it to one of the least of these who are members of my family, you did it to me.'"

- I can reflect on my life and see that whatever I did not do—and could have done—for others has also been neglect of Jesus. What I did for others is help for Jesus.
- Prayer gives an awareness of Jesus's presence and need in ordinary circumstances. Allow today, yesterday, or last week to come into prayer, simply by asking where today (or yesterday, or last week) did I answer or ignore a legitimate call of Jesus for help.
- See the scene in prayer and try to sense or picture that Jesus is there saying, "This is me, here and now."

**Tuesday 19th February Matthew 6:7–15**

Jesus said, "When you are praying, do not heap up empty phrases as the Gentiles do; for they think that they will be heard because of their many words. Do not be like them, for your Father knows what you need before you ask him. Pray then in this way: Our Father in heaven, hallowed be your name. Your kingdom come. Your will be done, on earth as it is in heaven. Give us this day our daily bread. And forgive us our debts, as we also have forgiven our debtors. And do not bring us to the time of trial, but rescue us from the evil one. For if you forgive others their trespasses, your heavenly Father will also forgive you; but if you do not forgive others, neither will your Father forgive your trespasses."

- Jesus gives a model for prayer in the Our Father. I pray for those who taught it to me, for all who helped me to understand it.
- I take the prayer in the words that are familiar to me and pray that God's way of being and seeing be evident in me.

**Wednesday 20th February Luke 11:29–30**

When the crowds were increasing, he began to say, "This generation is an evil generation; it asks for a sign, but no sign will be given to it except the sign of Jonah. For just as Jonah became a sign to the people of Nineveh, so the Son of Man will be to this generation."

- Jesus sees that the people looked for great signs of God's presence and action and missed noticing that God's spirit was among them. I acknowledge that too often I am easily distracted and do not take note of where I might attend to God's presence.
- Where have I found true consolation and encouragement? Do I value the nourishment that may be available to me?

**Thursday 21st February** **Matthew 7:9–12**

Jesus said to the disciples, "Is there anyone among you who, if your child asks for bread, will give a stone? Or if the child asks for a fish, will give a snake? If you then, who are evil, know how to give good gifts to your children, how much more will your Father in heaven give good things to those who ask him! In everything do to others as you would have them do to you; for this is the law and the prophets."

- Aware of being in God's presence, I consider how my prayers have been answered in the past. As I note that not everything worked out as I initially wanted, I also realize that I have been blessed in many different ways.
- What do those around me need from me? Might I be blessing to them as I answer their prayers and consider their needs?

**Friday 22nd February** **Matthew 5:20–24**

Jesus said to his disciples, "For I tell you, unless your righteousness exceeds that of the scribes and Pharisees, you will never enter the kingdom of heaven. You have heard that it was said to those of ancient times, 'You shall not murder'; and 'whoever murders shall be liable to judgment.' But I say to you that if you are angry with a brother or sister, you will be liable to judgment; and if you insult a brother or sister, you will be liable to the council; and if you say, 'You fool,' you will be liable to the hell of fire. So when you are offering your gift at the altar, if you remember that your brother or sister has something against you, leave your gift there before the altar and go; first be reconciled to your brother or sister, and then come and offer your gift."

- Jesus calls us not to be neutral, but to use our energies for the healing of relationships.
- Are there hurts that hold me back, that cause resentment? If so, I ask for healing, and pray for those who have caused me pain. If not, I give thanks to God that I do not carry burdens of this kind.

**Saturday 23rd February Matthew 5:43–48**

Jesus said to the disciples, "You have heard that it was said, 'You shall love your neighbor and hate your enemy.' But I say to you, Love your enemies and pray for those who persecute you, so that you may be children of your Father in heaven; for he makes his sun rise on the evil and on the good, and sends rain on the righteous and on the unrighteous. For if you love those who love you, what reward do you have? Do not even the tax collectors do the same?

And if you greet only your brothers and sisters, what more are you doing than others? Do not even the Gentiles do the same? Be perfect, therefore, as your heavenly Father is perfect."

- As I pray for those who bring blessings to me, I pray that I may include others in a widening circle of compassion.
- If being like God seems too ambitious, I recall that Jesus wants nothing less for me. He calls me to the fullness of life.

# february 24–march 2

Something to think and pray about each day this week:

**Discerning the Call**

Lord, I believe you are calling me in all the circumstances of my life, but there are times when your hand is difficult to recognize. The calling can sometimes come in a disagreeable shape, a sickness, bereavement, betrayal, loss of a job, a bout of insecurity. It does not look like a vocation but rather an unfortunate accident, or a failure on my part. But success is what I do with my failures. Each step on the way is part of God's calling. How do I handle deep distress?

**The Presence of God**

For a few moments, I think of God's veiled presence in things:
in the elements, giving them existence;
in plants, giving them life; in animals, giving them sensation;
and finally, in me, giving me all this and more,
making me a temple, a dwelling-place of the Spirit.

**Freedom**

God is not foreign to my freedom.
Instead the Spirit breathes life into my most intimate desires,
gently nudging me towards all that is good.
I ask for the grace to let myself be enfolded by the Spirit.

**Consciousness**

Knowing that God loves me unconditionally,
I can afford to be honest about how I am.
How has the last day been, and how do I feel now?
I share my feelings openly with the Lord.

**The Word**

The Word of God comes down to us through the scriptures. May the Holy Spirit enlighten my mind and my heart to respond to the gospel teachings. (Please turn to your scripture on the following pages. Inspiration points are there should you need them. When you are ready, return here to continue.)

**Conversation**

How has God's Word moved me? Has it left me cold?

Has it consoled me or moved me to act in a new way?

I imagine Jesus standing or sitting beside me,

I turn and share my feelings with him.

**Conclusion**

Glory be to the Father, and to the Son, and to the Holy Spirit,

As it was in the beginning, is now and ever shall be,

World without end. Amen.

**Sunday 24th February,**
**Second Sunday of Lent** **Luke 9:28–36**

Now about eight days after these sayings Jesus took with him Peter and John and James, and went up on the mountain to pray. And while he was praying, the appearance of his face changed, and his clothes became dazzling white. Suddenly they saw two men, Moses and Elijah, talking to him. They appeared in glory and were speaking of his departure, which he was about to accomplish at Jerusalem. Now Peter and his companions were weighed down with sleep; but since they had stayed awake, they saw his glory and the two men who stood with him. Just as they were leaving him, Peter said to Jesus, "Master, it is good for us to be here; let us make three dwellings, one for you, one for Moses, and one for Elijah"—not knowing what he said.

While he was saying this, a cloud came and overshadowed them; and they were terrified as they entered the cloud. Then from the cloud came a voice that said, "This is my Son, my Chosen; listen to him!" When the voice had spoken, Jesus was found alone. And they kept silent and in those days told no one any of the things they had seen.

- Jesus chose Peter, James, and John to witness his glory before he faced the Passion. It woke them up, this mysterious and memorable moment on Mount Tabor.
- Thank you, Lord, for the moments when I feel you close to me. They strengthen me to face the desolate lowlands of my life.

**Monday 25th February** **Luke 6:36–38**

Be merciful, just as your Father is merciful. Do not judge, and you will not be judged; do not condemn, and you will not be condemned. Forgive, and you will be forgiven; give, and it will be given to you. A good measure, pressed down, shaken together, running over, will be put into your lap; for the measure you give will be the measure you get back."

- I ask God to continue to soften my heart to make me more compassionate, more merciful. I recognize that I am already able to show some forgiveness and ask God's help with this.
- "Forgive us our sins as we forgive those . . ." As I ask God for forgiveness, I make room in my heart not just by letting go of hurts, but by wishing well to any who may have brought me pain.

**Tuesday 26th February Matthew 23:1, 9–12**

Then Jesus said to the crowds and to his disciples, "Call no one your father on earth, for you have one Father—the one in heaven. Nor are you to be called instructors, for you have one instructor, the Messiah. The greatest among you will be your servant. All who exalt themselves will be humbled, and all who humble themselves will be exalted."

- It is easy to be distracted by fame, celebrity, or royalty. I think of how my real dignity—my true identity—lies in my being a child of God. I consider how I might live in a way that brings others to the fullness of their dignity.
- Jesus took on the role of servant and continues to serve me. I ask for the grace I need to serve humbly.

**Wednesday 27th February Matthew 20:20–28**

Then the mother of the sons of Zebedee came to him with her sons, and kneeling before him, she asked a favor of him. And he said to her, "What do you want?" She said to him, "Declare that these two sons of mine will sit, one at your right hand and one at your left, in your kingdom." But Jesus answered, "You do not know what you are asking. Are you able to drink the cup that I am about to drink?" They said to him, "We are able." He said to them, "You will indeed drink my cup, but to sit at my right hand and at my left, this is not mine to grant, but it is for those for whom it has been prepared by my Father." When the ten heard it, they were angry with the two brothers. But Jesus called them to him and said, "You know that the rulers of the Gentiles lord it over them, and their great ones are tyrants over them. It will not be so among you; but whoever wishes to be great among you must be your servant, and whoever wishes to be first among you must be your slave; just as the Son of Man came not to be served but to serve, and to give his life a ransom for many."

- Even though the disciples lived closely with Jesus, it took some a long time to grow into an understanding of his vision. I realize that Jesus recognizes that I too can be slow to understand, and allow myself to experience his compassionate, loving gaze.
- As I realize how the other apostles were angry with James and John, I ask Jesus to help me to be patient and forgiving of those disciples who do not see things as I do.

**Thursday 28th February** **Luke 16:19–31**

Jesus said to the Pharisees, "There was a rich man who was dressed in purple and fine linen and who feasted sumptuously every day. And at his gate lay a poor man named Lazarus, covered with sores, who longed to satisfy his hunger with what fell from the rich man's table; even the dogs would come and lick his sores. The poor man died and was carried away by the angels to be with Abraham. The rich man also died and was buried. In Hades, where he was being tormented, he looked up and saw Abraham far away with Lazarus by his side. He called out, 'Father Abraham, have mercy on me, and send Lazarus to dip the tip of his finger in water and cool my tongue; for I am in agony in these flames.' But Abraham said, 'Child, remember that during your lifetime you received your good things, and Lazarus in like manner evil things; but now he is comforted here, and you are in agony. Besides all this, between you and us a great chasm has been fixed, so that those who might want to pass from here to you cannot do so, and no one can cross from there to us.' He said, 'Then, father, I beg you to send him to my father's house—for I have five brothers—that he may warn them, so that they will not also come into this place of torment.' Abraham replied, 'They have Moses and the prophets; they should listen to them.' He said, 'No, father Abraham; but if someone goes to them from the dead, they will repent.' He said to him, 'If they do not listen to Moses and the prophets, neither will they be convinced even if someone rises from the dead.'"

- During Lent, I try to hear the call to come back home to God. I join the great pilgrimage of people who, throughout the ages, have been called by Moses and the prophets to listen to the word of the Lord.
- I ask for a greater sensitivity to those who live with nothing, and I think of how I

might show some compassion to those whose need is greater than mine.

**Friday 1st March** **Matthew 21:33–41**

Jesus said, "Listen to another parable. There was a landowner who planted a vineyard, put a fence around it, dug a wine press in it, and built a watch-tower. Then he leased it to tenants and went to another country. When the harvest time had come, he sent his slaves to the tenants to collect his produce. But the tenants seized his slaves and beat one, killed another, and stoned another. Again he sent other slaves, more than the first; and they treated them in the same way. Finally he sent his son to them, saying, 'They will respect my son.' But when the tenants saw the son, they said to themselves, 'This is the heir; come, let us kill him and get his inheritance.' So they seized him, threw him out of the vineyard, and killed him. Now when the owner of the vineyard comes, what will he do to those tenants?" They said to him, "He will put those wretches to a miserable death, and lease the vineyard to other tenants who will give him the produce at the harvest time."

- Just as the landlord planted, protected, nourished, and guarded his property, so has God attended to my needs.
- I think of how I am made to give glory to God. I give thanks as I realize that the goodness of God can be seen in my life. I ask forgiveness as I acknowledge that I, like the tenants in the parable, sometimes prefer to run things in my own way.

**Saturday 2nd March** **Luke 15:21–24**

Then the son said to him, "Father, I have sinned against heaven and before you; I am no longer worthy to be called your son." But the father said to his slaves, "Quickly, bring out a robe—the best one—and put it on him; put a ring on his finger and sandals on his feet. And get the fatted calf and kill it, and let us eat and celebrate; for this son of mine was dead and is alive again; he was lost and is found!" And they began to celebrate.

- Jesus was criticized for associating with sinners and the unworthy. I remind myself that I do not earn Jesus's grace by my prayer or by my action. Jesus wants to be with me to bring me fullness of life.
- Even though I may not feel worthy, I listen for the voice of God recognizing me, welcoming me, loving me, lavishing me with the best of gifts: the ring reminds me of my dignity and the sandals tell me that I am free.

# march 3–9

Something to think and pray about each day this week:

**The Mystery of Conversion**

There is a legend of how Saint Patrick, when preaching to some soon-to-be converted heathens, was shown a sacred standing stone marked with a circle that was symbolic of the moon goddess. Patrick made the mark of a Latin cross through the circle and blessed the stone, making the first Celtic Cross. This legend implies that the Saint was willing to recast formerly Druid ideas and practices as Christian. The circle of the Celtic Cross is a symbol of eternity that emphasizes the endlessness of God's love as shown through Christ's sacrifice on the Cross—or the circle may be seen as a halo. The crucifixion is important, and not just as an event at a certain point in time. The circle symbolizes the unending mystery of how, through the crucifixion and resurrection, Christ continues to offer the hope of salvation to the faithful throughout all time.

**The Presence of God**

Dear Jesus, today I call on you in a special way.
Mostly I come asking for favors.
Today I'd like just to be in Your presence.
Let my heart respond to Your Love.

**Freedom**

'I am free.'
When I look at these words in writing,
They seem to create in me a feeling of awe.
Yes, a wonderful feeling of freedom.

Thank You, God.

**Consciousness**

Lord, you gave me the night to rest in sleep.
In my waking hours may I not forget your goodness to me.
Guide me to share your blessings with others.

**The Word**

I read the Word of God slowly, a few times over, and I listen to what God is saying to me. (Please turn to your scripture on the following pages. Inspiration points are there should you need them. When you are ready, return here to continue.)

**Conversation**

Dear Jesus, I can open up my heart to you.
I can tell you everything that troubles me.

I know you care about all the concerns in my life.
Teach me to live in the knowledge
that you who care for me today,
will care for me tomorrow, and all the days of my life.

**Conclusion**

Glory be to the Father, and to the Son,
and to the Holy Spirit,
As it was in the beginning, is now and ever shall be,
World without end. Amen.

**Sunday 3rd March,**
**Third Sunday of Lent** **Luke 13:6–9**

Jesus told this parable: "A man had a fig tree planted in his vineyard; and he came looking for fruit on it and found none. So he said to the gardener, 'See here! For three years I have come looking for fruit on this fig tree, and still I find none. Cut it down! Why should it be wasting the soil?' He replied, 'Sir, let it alone for one more year, until I dig around it and put manure on it. If it bears fruit next year, well and good; but if not, you can cut it down.'"

- You look for fruit, Lord. We are not in this world just to absorb and take in. It is our job as your children to give something back.
- Nobody likes to be dug around and manured; but that unsought disturbance in my life can be God's way of helping me to bear fruit.

**Monday 4th March** **Luke 4:24–30**

And he said, "Truly I tell you, no prophet is accepted in the prophet's hometown. But the truth is, there were many widows in Israel in the time of Elijah, when the heaven was shut up three years and six months, and there was a severe famine over all the land; yet Elijah was sent to none of them except to a widow at Zarephath in Sidon. There were also many lepers in Israel in the time of the prophet Elisha, and none of them was cleansed except Naaman the Syrian." When they heard this, all in the synagogue were filled with rage. They got up, drove him out of the town, and led him to the brow of the hill on which their town was built, so that they might hurl him off the cliff. But he passed through the midst of them and went on his way.

- The people of Jesus's hometown had come to their conclusions; they left no room for Jesus to work in a new way.
- I bring my fixed ideas before God, that I may let go of them, praying that they not blind me to the movement of God's Spirit.

**Tuesday 5th March** **Matthew 18:21–22**

Then Peter came and said to him, "Lord, if another member of the church sins against me, how often should I forgive? As many as seven times?" Jesus said to him, "Not seven times, but, I tell you, seventy-seven times."

- As Jesus continues to emphasize forgiveness, I humbly bring myself before God who forgives me everything, who loves me beyond any sin. The forgiveness that God gives is often difficult for me to receive.

- I pray for those who have caused me hurt, and, even if I can't wish them well now, I pray that one day I might.

**Wednesday 6th March** **Matthew 5:17–19**

Jesus said to his disciples, "Do not think that I have come to abolish the law or the prophets; I have come not to abolish but to fulfill. For truly I tell you, until heaven and earth pass away, not one letter, not one stroke of a letter, will pass from the law until all is accomplished. Therefore, whoever breaks one of the least of these commandments, and teaches others to do the same, will be called least in the kingdom of heaven; but whoever does them and teaches them will be called great in the kingdom of heaven."

- I consider my way of living and my influence on others. I pray in thanksgiving for those places in my life where I can imagine that I have a good influence.

- I ask for God's help in the areas where my example and inspiration might be better.

**Thursday 7th March** **Luke 11:14–20**

Jesus was casting out a demon that was mute; when the demon had gone out, the one who had been mute spoke, and the crowds were amazed. But some of them said, "He casts out demons by Beelzebul, the ruler of the demons." Others, to test him, kept demanding from him a sign from heaven. But he knew what they were thinking and said to them, "Every kingdom divided against itself becomes a desert, and house falls on house. If Satan also is divided against himself, how will his kingdom stand?—for you say that I cast out the demons by Beelzebul. Now if I cast out the demons by Beelzebul, by whom do your exorcists cast them out? Therefore they will be your judges. But if it is by the finger of God that I cast out the demons, then the kingdom of God has come to you."

- The people who criticized Jesus focused on the demons, not on the one who sought to banish them. Sometimes I become preoccupied by negative details, by failures and disappointments. I ask Jesus to help me during this Lent to realize that he calls me away from any ill that holds me back.
- As I realize how I need to reform my life during Lent, I remember not to depend on my own efforts, but learn to rely on Jesus who gathers me together.

**Friday 8th March** **Mark 12:28–34**

One of the scribes came near and heard them disputing with one another, and seeing that he answered them well, he asked him, "Which commandment is the first of all?" Jesus answered, "The first is, 'Hear, O Israel: the Lord our God, the Lord is one; you shall love the Lord your God with all your heart, and with all your soul, and with all your mind, and with all your strength.' The second is this, 'You shall love your neighbor as yourself.' There is no other commandment greater than these." Then the scribe said to him, "You are right, Teacher; you have truly said that 'he is one, and besides him there is no other'; and 'to love him with all the heart, and with all the understanding, and with all the strength,' and 'to love one's neighbor as oneself,'— this is much more important than all whole burnt offerings and sacrifices." When Jesus saw that he answered wisely, he said to him, "You are not far from the kingdom of

God." After that no one dared to ask him any question.

- Jesus recites the "Shema Israel," the prayer that he knew from his earliest years. As I am at prayer, I give God thanks for my own history of prayer, recalling those who taught me and giving thanks for all who have helped me to hear the voice of the Lord.
- I consider how my love for myself and my love for my neighbor might be brought into a better balance this Lent.

**Saturday 9th March** **Luke 18:9–14**

He also told this parable to some who trusted in themselves that they were righteous and regarded others with contempt: "Two men went up to the temple to pray, one a Pharisee and the other a tax collector. The Pharisee, standing by himself, was praying thus, 'God, I thank you that I am not like other people: thieves, rogues, adulterers, or even like this tax collector. I fast twice a week; I give a tenth of all my income.' But the tax collector, standing far off, would not even look up to heaven, but was beating his breast and saying, 'God, be merciful to me, a sinner!' I tell you, this man went down to his home justified rather than the other; for all who exalt themselves will be humbled, but all who humble themselves will be exalted."

- There is probably both a Pharisee and a Tax Collector right in my heart; at times arrogant, at times weak and uncertain.
- Do I have difficulty asking God for mercy on my sinfulness?
- Jesus says that the weak and vulnerable person who is honest about their weakness and vulnerability is the one who is truly free.

## march 10–16

Something to think and pray about each day this week:

**The Christian Struggle**

Can you imagine sailing against a head wind on a stormy sea? Tension is high. You've got to be alert, concentrated, steadfast, and energetic in setting yourself against the ongoing challenge. It's tough, but it's also exhilarating, exciting, and deeply satisfying to know you're on course despite the elements' efforts to upturn you!

Lent invites us to re-engage with the Christian struggle, to face the enemy within (our tendency to sin) and without (elements of our culture that are un-loving, un-Christian), and boldly fix our eyes on the goal, the prize of true freedom. The struggle can be tough and demanding, but it brings with it a wonderful sense of well-being and fulfilment. God confirms our efforts and encourages us along the way—his Way, the way of truth.

Let us be attentive to the voice of our Captain this Lent. Let us listen to his Word, his advice, his instruction. It will surely bring wisdom, courage, consolation, and great joy into our lives.

**The Presence of God**

In the silence of my innermost being,
in the fragments of my yearned-for wholeness,
can I hear the whispers of God's presence?
Can I remember when I felt God's nearness?

When we walked together and I let myself
be embraced by God's love?

**Freedom**

There are very few people
who realize what God would make of
them
if they abandoned themselves into his
hands,
and let themselves be formed by his grace.
(St. Ignatius)
I ask for the grace to trust myself totally to
God's love.

**Consciousness**

How do I find myself today?
Where am I with God? With others?
Do I have something to be grateful for?
Then, I give thanks.
Is there something I am sorry for? Then, I
ask forgiveness.

**The Word**

I take my time to read the Word of God, slowly, a few times, allowing myself to dwell on anything that strikes me.

(Please turn to your scripture on the following pages. Inspiration points are there should you need them. When you are ready, return here to continue.)

**Conversation**

Do I notice myself reacting as I pray with the Word of God?

Do I feel challenged, comforted, angry?

Imagining Jesus sitting or standing by me, I speak out my feelings, as one trusted friend to another.

**Conclusion**

Glory be to the Father, and to the Son,
and to the Holy Spirit,
As it was in the beginning, is now and ever shall be,
World without end. Amen.

**Sunday 10th March,**
**Fourth Sunday of Lent 2 Corinthians 5:17–20**

So if anyone is in Christ, there is a new creation: everything old has passed away; see, everything has become new! All this is from God, who reconciled us to himself through Christ, and has given us the ministry of reconciliation; that is, in Christ God was reconciling the world to himself, not counting their trespasses against them, and entrusting the message of reconciliation to us. So we are ambassadors for Christ, since God is making his appeal through us; we entreat you on behalf of Christ, be reconciled to God.

- Ambassadors for Christ, in a ministry of reconciliation. It is a simple mission, one that is never accomplished, but is sustained by the joy of being Jesus's ambassador.

**Monday 11th March** **John 4:46b–54**

Now there was a royal official whose son lay ill in Capernaum. When he heard that Jesus had come from Judea to Galilee, he went and begged him to come down and heal his son, for he was at the point of death. Then Jesus said to him, "Unless you see signs and wonders you will not believe." The official said to him, "Sir, come down before my little boy dies." Jesus said to him, "Go; your son will live." The man believed the word that Jesus spoke to him and started on his way. As he was going down, his slaves met him and told him that his child was alive. So he asked them the hour when he began to recover, and they said to him, "Yesterday at one in the afternoon the fever left him." The father realized that this was the hour when Jesus had said to him, "Your son will live." So he himself believed, along with his whole household. Now this was the second sign that Jesus did after coming from Judea to Galilee.

- "Your son will live," said Jesus, who was coming ever closer to his own death, his "hour." This foreshadowing points toward the new life, the new creation that is to come.
- Like the boy's father, can I believe—can I put my trust in God?

**Tuesday 12th March** **John 5:2–9**

Now in Jerusalem by the Sheep Gate there is a pool, called in Hebrew Beth-zatha, which has five porticoes. In these lay many invalids—blind, lame, and paralyzed. One man was there who had been ill for thirty-eight years. When Jesus saw him lying there and knew that he had been there a long time, he said to him, "Do you want to be made well?" The sick man answered him, "Sir, I have no one to put me into the pool when the water is stirred up; and while I am making my way, someone else steps down ahead of me." Jesus said to him, "Stand up, take your mat and walk." At once the man was made well, and he took up his mat and began to walk.

- The sick man did not answer Jesus's question, but told the familiar story of his troubles.
- As Jesus now speaks to me, I do my best to answer what he asks, being careful not to rehearse any disempowering message.

**Wednesday 13th March John 5:24–25**

Jesus said to the Jews, "Very truly, I tell you, anyone who hears my word and believes him who sent me has eternal life, and does not come under judgment, but has passed from death to life. Very truly, I tell you, the hour is coming, and is now here, when the dead will hear the voice of the Son of God, and those who hear will live."

- Here Jesus is letting me in on the secret. As well as being the man who heals and teaches, he is much more.
- Am I open to the knowledge that Jesus is the way to eternal life? If I have difficulty understanding it, I can ask for insight.

**Thursday 14th March** **John 5:31–36**

Jesus said to the Jews, "If I testify about myself, my testimony is not true. There is another who testifies on my behalf, and I know that his testimony to me is true. You sent messengers to John, and he testified to the truth. Not that I accept such human testimony, but I say these things so that you may be saved. He was a burning and shining lamp, and you were willing to rejoice for a while in his light. But I have a testimony greater than John's."

- Jesus appeals to the minds of those who seek to disregard him. He reminds them of what they have seen, of the witnesses they have heard, and of the words of the prophets.
- I pray that I am blessed with deeper faith as I "review the evidence" to which Jesus draws my attention.
- As I believe in Jesus who was sent by God, the Word of God is alive me. I can give witness to this Word in my deeds and speech.

**Friday 15th March** **John 7:25–27**

Now some of the people of Jerusalem were saying, "Is not this the man whom they are trying to kill? And here he is, speaking openly, but they say nothing to him! Can it be that the authorities really know that this is the Messiah? Yet we know where this man is from; but when the Messiah comes, no one will know where he is from."

- They want an excuse not to believe. They want to be able to say, "this is not the Christ." So they focus on where he came from and say that the Christ will come from where nobody knows.
- "They" are "we"! It is human to find excuses not to believe, not to accept, not to follow God in Jesus. We bring these blocks within ourselves to prayer, and ask that our hardness of heart may be softened by faith. Teach us that we do not have to have an answer to everything.

**Saturday 16th March** **John 7:40–44**

When they heard these words, some in the crowd said, "This is really the prophet." Others said, "This is the Messiah." But some asked, "Surely the Messiah does not come from Galilee, does he? Has not the scripture said that the Messiah is descended from David and comes from Bethlehem, the village where David lived?" So there was a division in the crowd because of him. Some of them wanted to arrest him, but no one laid hands on him.

- Some people who heard Jesus could not believe that God might work powerfully in such ordinary and familiar circumstances.
- I pray that I may look again at my own situation, realizing that God is already at work even as I pray for an increase in God's grace.

# march 17–23

Something to think and pray about each day this week:

**Learning in Life**

This week the Church remembers St. Joseph, husband of Mary and foster-father of Jesus. Sartre, in his Christmas play *Bar-jona,* tries to picture Joseph in the stable at Bethlehem. "I would not paint Joseph. I would show no more than a shadow at the back of the stable, and two shining eyes. For I do not know what to say about Joseph, and Joseph does not know what to say about himself. He adores, and is happy to adore, and he feels himself slightly out of it. I believe he suffers without admitting it. He suffers because he sees how much this woman whom he loves resembles God; how she is already at the side of God. For God has burst like a bomb into the intimacy of this family. Joseph and Mary are separated forever by this explosion of light. And I imagine that all through his life Joseph will be learning to accept this."

**The Presence of God**

I reflect for a moment on God's presence around me and in me.
Creator of the universe, the sun and the moon, the earth,
every molecule, every atom, everything that is:
God is in every beat of my heart. God is with me, now.

**Freedom**

A thick and shapeless tree-trunk would never believe

that it could become a statue, admired as a miracle of sculpture,
and would never submit itself to the chisel of the sculptor,
who sees by her genius what she can make of it. (St. Ignatius)
I ask for the grace to let myself be shaped by my loving Creator.

**Consciousness**

Knowing that God loves me unconditionally,
I look honestly over the last day, its events and my feelings.
Do I have something to be grateful for? Then, I give thanks.
Is there something I am sorry for? Then, I ask forgiveness.

**The Word**

I read the Word of God slowly, a few times over, and I listen to what God is saying to me. (Please turn to your scripture on the following pages. Inspiration points are there should you need them. When you are ready, return here to continue.)

**Conversation**

What is stirring in me as I pray?
Am I consoled, troubled, left cold?
I imagine Jesus himself standing or sitting at my side,
and share my feelings with him.

**Conclusion**

Glory be to the Father, and to the Son,
and to the Holy Spirit,
As it was in the beginning, is now and ever shall be,
World without end. Amen.

**Sunday 17th March,**
**Fifth Sunday of Lent** **John 8:2–11**

Early in the morning Jesus came again to the temple. All the people came to him and he sat down and began to teach them. The scribes and the Pharisees brought a woman who had been caught in adultery; and making her stand before all of them, they said to him, "Teacher, this woman was caught in the very act of committing adultery. Now in the law Moses commanded us to stone such women. Now what do you say?" They said this to test him, so that they might have some charge to bring against him. Jesus bent down and wrote with his finger on the ground. When they kept on questioning him, he straightened up and said to them, "Let anyone among you who is without sin be the first to throw a stone at her." And once again he bent down and wrote on the ground. When they heard it, they went away, one by one, beginning with the elders; and Jesus was left alone with the woman standing before him. Jesus straightened up and said to her, "Woman, where are they? Has no one condemned you?" She said, "No one, sir." And Jesus said, "Neither do I condemn you. Go your way, and from now on do not sin again."

- Where do I stand in this scene? Like the woman standing before her accusers? Like a silent sympathizer hoping that something will happen to save her? Like the skulking male adulterer who got her into this trouble? Like the bystanders already collecting the best stones with a view to a killing? Like one of the elders who slink away, unable to cast the first stone?
- What goes through my head as Jesus is doodling in the sand?

**Monday 18th March Daniel 13:55–56, 60–62**

Daniel said, "Indeed! Your lie recoils on you own head: the angel of God has already received from him your sentence and will cut you in half." He dismissed the man, ordered the other to be brought and said to him, "Son of Canaan, not of Judah, beauty has seduced you, lust has led your heart astray!" . . . Then the whole assembly shouted, blessing God, the Savior of those who trust in him. And they turned on the two elders whom Daniel had convicted of false evidence out of their own mouths. As the Law of Moses prescribes, they were given the same punishment as they had schemed to inflict on their neighbor. They were put to death. And thus, that day, an innocent life was saved.

- These are not happy characters. Dissipation and addiction are forms of imprisonment in which the chains are inside you, not outside, so the pain is greater. The German ("God is dead") philosopher Nietzsche stated the downside of lust: "The mother of dissipation is not joy, but joylessness." Thomas Aquinas put it more positively: "A joyful heart is a sure sign of temperance and self-control." Do I show that sign?

**Tuesday 19th March,**
**St. Joseph** **Matthew 1:18–25**

Now the birth of Jesus the Messiah took place in this way. When his mother Mary had been engaged to Joseph, but before they lived together, she was found to be with child from the Holy Spirit. Her husband Joseph, being a righteous man and unwilling to expose her to public disgrace, planned to dismiss her quietly. But just when he had resolved to do this, an angel of the Lord appeared to him in a dream and said, "Joseph, son of David, do not be afraid to take Mary as your wife, for the child conceived in her is from the Holy Spirit. She will bear a son, and you are to name him Jesus, for he will save his people from their sins." All this took place to fulfill what had been spoken by the Lord through the prophet: "Look, the virgin shall conceive and bear a son, and they shall name him Emmanuel," which means, "God is with us." When Joseph awoke from sleep, he did as the angel of the Lord commanded him; he took her as his wife, but had no marital relations with her until she had borne a son; and he named him Jesus.

- We see Joseph as a sensitive person, careful not to bring dishonor on Mary and attending to the message of his dreams. There may be situations I need to avoid, and conditions

I need to create, to become more sensitive to the quiet movements of God's spirit.

- Joseph did not have much to go on, but he trusted his intuition, discerning in it the hand of God. I consider where in my life I have been blessed by trusting in God.

**Wednesday 20th March** **John 8:31–42**

Then Jesus said to the Jews who had believed in him, "If you continue in my word, you are truly my disciples; and you will know the truth, and the truth will make you free." They answered him, "We are descendants of Abraham and have never been slaves to anyone. What do you mean by saying, 'You will be made free'?" Jesus answered them, "Very truly, I tell you, everyone who commits sin is a slave to sin. The slave does not have a permanent place in the household; the son has a place there forever.

So if the Son makes you free, you will be free indeed. I know that you are descendants of Abraham; yet you look for an opportunity to kill me, because there is no place in you for my word. I declare what I have seen in the Father's presence; as for you, you should do what you have heard from the Father." They answered him, "Abraham is our father." Jesus said to them, "If you were Abraham's children, you would be doing what Abraham did, but now you are trying to kill me, a man who has told you the truth that I heard from God. This is not what Abraham did. You are indeed doing what your father does." They said to him, "We are not illegitimate children; we have one father, God himself." Jesus said to them, "If God were your Father, you would love me, for I came from God and now I am here. I did not come on my own, but he sent me."

- Jesus' hearers were stuck in their sense of themselves, in the pride they took in their heritage. Perhaps I can admit that I too have sometimes climbed the wrong heights—have congratulated myself mistakenly. I know that my true dignity lives in my being a child of God.
- I pray that I may show my true worth in how I live and call others to a deeper and richer sense of themselves.

**Thursday 21st March** **John 8:54–59**

Jesus said to the Jews, "If I glorify myself, my glory is nothing. It is my Father who glorifies me, he of whom you say, 'He is our God,' though you do not know him. But I know him; if I were to say that I do not know him, I would be a liar like you. But I do know him and I keep his word. Your ancestor Abraham rejoiced that he would see my day; he saw it and was glad." Then the Jews said to him, "You are not yet fifty years old, and have you seen Abraham?" Jesus said to them, "Very truly, I tell you, before Abraham was, I am." So they picked up stones to throw at him, but Jesus hid himself and went out of the temple.

- We keep the words of loved ones in our hearts, like their photos in a precious place. Or when we see them on a DVD or a video, we find love and memories coming alive. The Word of God is the same; it enlivens our souls and our convictions about what is best in life.
- Prayer brings us deeply into the words of God that mean a lot to us. God's word in Jesus keeps our faith alive, and his Word, who is Jesus, will be with us forever.

**Friday 22nd March** **John 10:31–40**

The Jews took up stones again to stone him. Jesus replied, "I have shown you many good works from the Father. For which of these are you going to stone me?" The Jews answered, "It is not for a good work that we are going to stone you, but for blasphemy, because you, though only a human being, are making yourself God." Jesus answered, "Is it not written in your law, 'I said, you are gods'? If those to whom the Word of God came were called 'gods'—and the scripture cannot be annulled—can you say that the one whom the Father has sanctified and sent into the world is blaspheming because I said, 'I am God's Son'? If I am not doing the works of my Father, then do not believe me. But if I do them, even though you do not believe me, believe the works, so that you may know and understand that the Father is in me and I am in the Father."

- Jesus was not putting himself above the people, but was calling them to realize their true worth.
- I think of how Jesus was born and became like me so that I may know myself truly as he accompanies me.

**Saturday 23rd March** **John 11:47–52**

So the chief priests and the Pharisees called a meeting of the council, and said, "What are we to do? This man is performing many signs. If we let him go on like this, everyone will believe in him, and the Romans will come and destroy both our holy place and our nation." But one of them, Caiaphas, who was high priest that year, said to them, "You know nothing at all! You do not understand that it is better for you to have one man die for the people than to have the whole nation destroyed." He did not say this on his own, but being high priest that year he prophesied that Jesus was about to die for the nation, and not for the nation only, but to gather into one the dispersed children of God.

- As we approach Holy Week, we consider how Jesus faced the prospect of arrest and condemnation.
- I pray that I may always do as Jesus did, considering how he took time in quiet, was with his friends and chose the times in which to speak and those in which to stay silent. Lord, help me find the proper balance, neither complicating issues nor thinking everything simple.

# march 24–30

Something to think and pray about each day this week:

**At the Tipping Point**

We have just passed the Equinox: night is as long as day, and we are half-way to summer or winter, depending on where we live. Where am I in my life? Past the equinox? In Andrew Marvell's words:

> But at my back I always hear
> Time's wingèd chariot hurrying
> near.

Lord, I cannot find you in time past or time future; only in this present moment. Teach me to use it to the full. That use may be writing or sleeping or loving or talking or playing or working—or praying. It is no use looking before and after and pining for what is not. The now is all I have. It is a sacrament, a sign of inward grace. A friend who came close to death once said that as she felt God's love sweep irresistibly over her, all the past, its achievements and its failures, became irrelevant. It is only in this moment that I can come close to God.

**Calvary's Victory**

Holy Week is unlike any other week in the Church's year. It begins with the illusory triumph of Palm Sunday, when Jesus is hailed as a celebrity in his own city of Jerusalem. It leads through the betrayal of Judas (remembered on Spy Wednesday), and the farewells of Thursday (called Maundy Thursday after the *Mandatum*, the command to love one another), the humiliations, tortures, and death on Good Friday, to the victory over death on Resurrection Morning. Nearly every human life will include some of those experiences. This week we can identify with the Lord each step of the way from the Mount of Olives to Calvary. When it comes to the Resurrection, the imagination boggles, yet it is the center of our faith. Lord, teach me to love my face and body, my temple of the Holy Spirit. It will grow old and die with me, but that is not the end. My body is sacred, and Easter opens a window for it and me onto a mysterious but endless vista.

**The Presence of God**

In the silence of my innermost being,
in the fragments of my yearned-for wholeness,
can I hear the whispers of God's presence?
Can I remember when I felt God's nearness?
When we walked together and I let myself be embraced by God's love.

**Freedom**

There are very few people
who realize what God would make of them
if they abandoned themselves into his hands,
and let themselves be formed by his grace.
(St. Ignatius)

I ask for the grace to trust myself totally to God's love.

**Consciousness**

How do I find myself today?
Where am I with God? With others?
Do I have something to be grateful for?
Then, I give thanks.
Is there something I am sorry for? Then, I ask forgiveness.

**The Word**

I take my time to read the Word of God,
slowly, a few times, allowing myself to

dwell on anything that strikes me. (Please turn to your scripture on the following pages. Inspiration points are there should you need them. When you are ready, return here to continue.)

**Conversation**

Do I notice myself reacting as I pray with the Word of God?
Do I feel challenged, comforted, angry?
Imagining Jesus sitting or standing by me, I speak out my feelings, as one trusted friend to another.

**Conclusion**

Glory be to the Father, and to the Son, and to the Holy Spirit,
As it was in the beginning, is now and ever shall be,
World without end. Amen.

**Sunday 24th March, Palm Sunday of the Lord's Passion** **Philippians 2:5–11**

Let the same mind be in you that was in Christ Jesus, who, though he was in the form of God, did not regard equality with God as something to be exploited, but emptied himself, taking the form of a slave, being born in human likeness. And being found in human form, he humbled himself and became obedient to the point of death—even death on a cross. Therefore God also highly exalted him and gave him the name that is above every name, so that at the name of Jesus every knee should bend, in heaven and on earth and under the earth, and every tongue should confess that Jesus Christ is Lord, to the glory of God the Father.

- This hymn expresses the depth of the mystery—that Jesus's inmost nature was divine, but still he emptied himself and took on a human form. He entered our humanity, completely.
- Lord, lead me further into this mystery: today and in this week to come.

**Monday 25th March** **John 12:1–6**

Six days before the Passover Jesus came to Bethany, the home of Lazarus, whom he had raised from the dead. There they gave a dinner for him. Martha served, and Lazarus was one of those at the table with him. Mary took a pound of costly perfume made of pure nard, anointed Jesus' feet, and wiped them with her hair. The house was filled with the fragrance of the perfume. But

Judas Iscariot, one of his disciples (the one who was about to betray him), said, "Why was this perfume not sold for three hundred denarii and the money given to the poor?" (He said this not because he cared about the poor, but because he was a thief; he kept the common purse and used to steal what was put into it.)

- Mary was able to be extravagantly generous and was not held back by the opinions of those around her. I can reflect her generosity and God's goodness to me by how I share my property, my goodwill, my love, and my forgiveness.
- I picture the house filled with perfume and imagine the fragrance of the good that I do permeating my surroundings.

**Tuesday 26th March John 13:31–33, 36–38**

When Judas had gone out, Jesus said, "Now the Son of Man has been glorified, and God has been glorified in him. If God has been glorified in him, God will also glorify him in himself and will glorify him at once. Little children, I am with you only a little longer. You will look for me; and as I said to the Jews so now I say to you, 'Where I am going, you cannot come.'" Simon Peter said to him, "Lord, where are you going?" Jesus answered, "Where I am going, you cannot follow me now; but you will follow afterwards." Peter said to him, "Lord, why can I not follow you now? I will lay down my life for you." Jesus answered, "Will you lay down your life for me? Very truly, I tell you, before the cock crows, you will have denied me three times."

- Enthusiasm did not allow Peter to be calculating or measured. I pray for the same willingness to follow Jesus boldly, even as I know that I also need the courage and resolve that would fail Peter in the difficult hour.
- Peter's denials were matched by his professions of faith. I prepare myself to walk with Jesus on his way of the cross by recalling how I have been strong and by asking for forgiveness for my weakness.

**Wednesday 27th March Matthew 26:14–16, 20–25**

Then one of the twelve, who was called Judas Iscariot, went to the chief priests and said, "What will you give me if I betray him to you?" They paid him thirty pieces of silver. And from that moment he began to look for an opportunity to betray him. When it was evening, Jesus took his place with the twelve; and while they were eating, he said, "Truly I tell you, one of you will betray me." And they became greatly distressed and began to say to him one after another, "Surely not I, Lord?" He answered, "The one who has dipped his hand into the bowl with me will betray me. The Son of Man goes as it is written of him, but woe to that one by whom the Son of Man is betrayed! It would have been better for that one not to have been born." Judas, who betrayed him, said, "Surely not I, Rabbi?" He replied, "You have said so."

- I ask for compassion for all who, like Judas, have been brought to a point of denial. I linger on the response of Jesus during these days of his trial.
- Aware of my own fragility, I ask Jesus for the strength that I need to give witness to his spirit in difficult moments.

**Thursday 28th March,**
**Holy Thursday** **John 13:2–15**

During supper Jesus, knowing that the Father had given all things into his hands, and that he had come from God and was going to God, got up from the table, took off his outer robe, and tied a towel around himself. Then he poured water into a basin and began to wash the disciples' feet and to wipe them with the towel that was tied around him. He came to Simon Peter, who said to him, "Lord, are you going to wash my feet?" Jesus answered, "You do not know now what I am doing, but later you will understand." Peter said to him, "You will never wash my feet." Jesus answered, "Unless I wash you, you have no share with me." Simon Peter said to him, "Lord, not my feet only but also my hands and my head!" Jesus said to him, "One who has bathed does not need to wash, except for the feet, but is entirely clean. And you are clean, though not all of you." For he knew who was to betray him; for this reason he said, "Not all of you are clean." After Jesus had washed their feet, had put on his robe, and had returned to the table, he said to them, "Do you know what I have done to you? You call me Teacher and Lord—and you are right, for that is what I am. So if I, your Lord and Teacher, have washed your feet, you also ought to wash one another's feet. For I have set you an example, that you also should do as I have done to you."

- Jesus knows who he is—where he has come from, where he is going. He is teaching his disciples that their true identity is to be servants of one another in his image. I ask to learn what I need to learn from this scene.

- How do I feel as I see him rise from the table and approach me, kneel before me, and prepare to wash my feet?

**Friday 29th March,**
**Good Friday** **John 19:25–30**

Meanwhile, standing near the cross of Jesus were his mother, and his mother's sister, Mary the wife of Clopas, and Mary Magdalene. When Jesus saw his mother and the disciple whom he loved standing beside her, he said to his mother, "Woman, here is your son." Then he said to the disciple, "Here is your mother." And from that hour the disciple took her into his own home. After this, when Jesus knew that all was now finished, he said (in order to fulfill the scripture), "I am thirsty." A jar full of sour wine was standing there. So they put a sponge full of the wine on a branch of hyssop and held it to his mouth. When Jesus had received the wine, he said, "It is finished." Then he bowed his head and gave up his spirit.

- There are four "acts" in the passion of Jesus: his arrest; his interrogation by the High Priest, his trial before Pilate; his crucifixion and burial. I watch him as he moves through these scenes. I observe how he seems gentle and calm, and look at the impact he has on others.
- I watch him subjected to disgraceful injustice and unspeakable torture and humiliation as he moves through his passion.

He does not protest or cry out. How do I respond to injustice, ill-treatment, humiliation in my own life? What can I learn from him?

**Saturday 30th March,**
**Holy Saturday** **Matthew 27:57–66**

When it was evening, there came a rich man from Arimathea, named Joseph, who was also a disciple of Jesus. He went to Pilate and asked for the body of Jesus; then Pilate ordered it to be given to him. So Joseph took the body and wrapped it in a clean linen cloth and laid it in his own new tomb, which he had hewn in the rock. He then rolled a great stone to the door of the tomb and went away. Mary Magdalene and the other Mary were there, sitting opposite the tomb. The next day, that is, after the day of Preparation, the chief priests and the

Pharisees gathered before Pilate and said, "Sir, we remember what that impostor said while he was still alive, 'After three days I will rise again.' Therefore command that the tomb be made secure until the third day; otherwise his disciples may go and steal him away, and tell the people, 'He has been raised from the dead', and the last deception would be worse than the first." Pilate said to them, "You have a guard of soldiers; go, make it as secure as you can." So they went with the guard and made the tomb secure by sealing the stone.

- I think of Pilate and Joseph of Arimathea in the presence of that dead body. Pilate had known Jesus was innocent, but, fearing for his own position, handed him over to death. Joseph had come to believe and hope in him as a disciple. Pilate wants to get rid of the body. Joseph receives it with deep reverence. I watch him place the body with great love and care in the tomb he had prepared for himself.

- Joseph goes away. I remain with Mary Magdalene and the other Mary, watching, waiting, and reflecting on what has happened over the past days.

# march 31

Something to think and pray about today:

**The Words of Love**

Lord, I envy the enthusiasm of the early disciples. They could not keep from speaking about what they had seen and heard. But I have not seen or heard it; and when I speak about your love, it sometimes sounds as though I have learned it out of a book. Yet I have felt you: sometimes in moments of anguish and incompleteness when I know that I am made for something beyond this; sometimes in moments of transcending joy, when I feel the glory of being loved. Give me words to do justice to my own experience.

**The Presence of God**

God is with me, but more,
God is within me, giving me existence.
Let me dwell for a moment on God's life-giving presence
in my body, my mind, my heart
and in the whole of my life.

**Freedom**

Many countries are at this moment suffering
the agonies of war.
I bow my head in thanksgiving for my freedom.
I pray for all prisoners and captives.

**Consciousness**

I remind myself that I am in the presence of the Lord.
I will take refuge in his loving heart.
He is my strength in times of weakness.
He is my comforter in times of sorrow.

**The Word**

I read the Word of God slowly, a few times over, and I listen to what God is saying to me. (Please turn to your scripture on the following pages. Inspiration points are there should you need them. When you are ready, return here to continue.)

**Conversation**

How has God's Word moved me? Has it left me cold?
Has it consoled me or moved me to act in a new way?
I imagine Jesus standing or sitting beside me,
I turn and share my feelings with him.

**Conclusion**

Glory be to the Father, and to the Son, and to the Holy Spirit,
As it was in the beginning, is now and ever shall be,
World without end. Amen.

**Sunday 31st March,**
**Easter Sunday** **John 20:1–9**

Early on the first day of the week, while it was still dark, Mary Magdalene came to the tomb and saw that the stone had been removed from the tomb. So she ran and went to Simon Peter and the other disciple, the one whom Jesus loved, and said to them, "They have taken the Lord out of the tomb, and we do not know where they have laid him." Then Peter and the other disciple set out and went toward the tomb. The two were running together, but the other disciple outran Peter and reached the tomb first. He bent down to look in and saw the linen wrappings lying there, but he did not go in. Then Simon Peter came, following him, and went into the tomb. He saw the linen wrappings lying there, and the cloth that had been on Jesus' head, not lying with the linen wrappings but rolled up in a place by itself. Then the other disciple, who reached the tomb first, also went in, and he saw and believed; for as yet they did not understand the scripture, that he must rise from the dead.

- It is the "first day of the week." Mary Magdalene is the first witness of an event which marks not just the beginning of a new week but the transformation of human history. But "it is still dark" and she does not yet understand what has happened. I ponder the mystery.
- Peter and the other disciple, who had stood faithfully beneath the cross, run to the tomb. The other disciple saw and believed. Peter, whose last recorded action was to deny Jesus, still does not believe. What blocks me from fuller faith?

Founded in 1865, Ave Maria Press, a ministry of the Congregation of Holy Cross, is a Catholic publishing company that serves the spiritual and formative needs of the Church and its schools, institutions, and ministers; Christian individuals and families; and others seeking spiritual nourishment.

For a complete listing of titles from

Ave Maria Press

Sorin Books

Forest of Peace

Christian Classics

visit www.avemariapress.com

ave maria press® / Notre Dame, IN 46556
A Ministry of the United States Province of Holy Cross